Original title:
The Treehouse Chronicles

Copyright © 2025 Creative Arts Management OÜ
All rights reserved.

Author: Julian Montgomery
ISBN HARDBACK: 978-1-80567-161-9
ISBN PAPERBACK: 978-1-80567-460-3

Serendipity in the Splendid Grove

In the grove where squirrels dance,
A nest of jokes awaits a chance.
The birds take flight with silly squawks,
While raccoons wear mismatched socks.

The haphazard flowers laugh and bloom,
As bees build dreams in their sweet room.
A frog, it seems, can tell a joke,
While owls stay up and just poke smoke.

Cradled in the Crooked Branches

A seat on branches, lopsided, hard,
Where gnomes convene and play their card.
They bet on leaves that flutter down,
And crown the mushroom as their crown.

The wind does cartwheels, spins and twirls,
While fireflies enact their curls.
A chicken joins in, struts with pride,
Clucking rhythms, a joyful ride.

Voyage of the Winds Through Wood

The winds embark on laughs and gales,
With whispered secrets, whims, and trails.
A snail with goggles glides right past,
While chipmunks tie their shoelaces fast.

They surf the breezes, in uproarious style,
As fungi giggle and grin a while.
The map is scribbled, but who needs that?
When every twist yields a tale so fat!

A Canvas of Color in the Canopy

A splash of hues from branches high,
Where laughter twinkles in the sky.
The pigments dance, the colors tease,
While bees paint stripes with zestful ease.

The sun paints smiles on leafy faces,
As creatures roam through vibrant spaces.
With a wink, the trees join in the jest,
Creating art in nature's quest.

Resilience of the Shelter Above

In a tree so high and spry,
Nuts fall like confetti from the sky.
Squirrels debate, should they stay or go?
With acorn plans, they put on a show.

Branches creak under our laughter's weight,
The raccoons join in, sharing their fate.
We dance with the leaves, oh what a sight,
As wind whispers secrets through day and night.

Pages Torn from Nature's Book

A beetle narrates tales of the day,
While ants march in lines, looking quite sway.
Insects host parties without any glue,
They serve up the nectar and hum a tune too.

Frogs hop about just seeking their fame,
Proclaiming their kingdom in the wild game.
With slime and with croaks, they read from the tome,
Nature's wild pages, a true froggy home.

Revelations Under a Canopy

Birds shoot by, with a chirpy cheer,
Dropping their wisdom, loud and clear.
"Eat more worms, they help you to fly!"
Is that wisdom, or just a good lie?

Beneath the wide leaves, we craft our schemes,
Plotting our heists like kids in dreams.
If we can just get that tree pie to bake,
We'll snack on delight, for goodness' sake!

A Grotto in the Branches

In a grotto high, where mischief resides,
Lizards hold court and gossip like tides.
They claim the best sunbathing spots,
While worms wiggle by, tying their knots.

Set up a stage made of twigs and leaves,
For jokes and fun that nobody believes.
A turtle, a snail, all grace this show,
With punchlines so slow, they steal the glow.

Sunlit Revelations Among the Leaves

In the branches we declare,
A kingdom made of sunlight and flair.
Squirrels gossip in a hurried dance,
While ants throw a grand balcony prance.

Laughter echoes from every nook,
While birds plot a surprise in their book.
A secret fort with a rope swing tight,
As we brainstorm ways to take flight.

A Bridge to the Sky

A ladder stretches, reaching high,
To a world where dreams dare to fly.
Beneath us, the ground spins in glee,
While we plan to conquer the tallest tree.

Bugs buzzing, singing their tunes,
We launch paper planes under shiny moons.
With every mishap, we just can't stop,
Making the branch our launching spot.

Splintered Light and Silent Secrets

Sunbeams peek through leafy veils,
Shining bright on our silly tales.
We sketch our dreams on rustic slats,
Engaging in battles with the neighbor's cats.

Whispers float from twig to wing,
As misplaced socks become the new king.
Together we build, we laugh, we slide,
Secrets hidden where the wild things hide.

Voices of the Wind in the Leaves

The wind carries whispers of unknown lore,
As we swing higher, hearts racing for more.
Giggles bubble up like a spring,
While the leaves take flight on a secret wing.

Cracking jokes about the sun's bright stare,
As we dare each other to climb up there.
Let's paint the world in hues of green,
And become the silliest crew ever seen.

Shadows of a Remembered Summer

In a hideout high, laughter flies,
Squirrels plot in whispered ties.
Sticky fingers on the treat,
Bouncing on that wobbly seat.

With branches creaky, swing so free,
We laugh at bugs that sting with glee.
Round and round the stories spin,
Where summer's glow is thick as sin.

Guardians of the Woodland Realm

In leafy halls, we claim our throne,
With crowns of twigs, we're never alone.
The owls hoot secrets, wise and sly,
While we scale trees, aiming for the sky.

Meeting a raccoon? It's quite a sight,
He steals our snacks, then darts from sight.
Our kingdom rules with childish pride,
In this green fortress, we safely hide.

Gaze from the Gnarled Limbs

From these gnarled limbs, we spy and sneak,
The squirrels chatter, and branches creak.
The sun grows dim, like evening tea,
As shadows dance, wild and free.

With roots so deep and tales so tall,
We turn our treehouse into a hall.
The world below, just a blur,
In this lofty life, we often stir.

A Kingdom in the Treetops

Our kingdom where the wild things roam,
Crafted out of dreams and frosty foam.
A dragon made from heaps of leaves,
Where time is fable, and laughter weaves.

Up among the chatter and chirps,
We play with magic, dodge the burps.
A spell of giggles fills the air,
In our treetop world, we have no care.

Memory Lane on High

Up in the branches, we laugh and play,
With squirrels above, having their ballet.
A slide made of leaves, oh what a sight,
We race down the trunk, hearts feeling light.

The world below sounds like a grand show,
While we munch on snacks, all safe in our glow.
A swing made of vines, we soar in the air,
The winds tease our hair, like they just don't care!

Raindrops and Revelations Above

Pitter patter, a shower of fun,
We're drenched and we giggle, pretending to run.
The trees are our shelter, a makeshift retreat,
With puddles like mirrors, we dance on our feet.

A drippy distraction, we concoct a scheme,
To catch all the raindrops, living the dream.
Our fortress of laughter, under the storm,
We crown each other with leaves, our hearts warm.

The World Beneath the Canopy

In our leafy palace, we spy on the ground,
As ants march in lines, all bustling around.
We toss down some acorns, a comical game,
To see if the creatures will play the same way.

A parade of surprises, a worm in a tie,
That much-debated beetle, oh my, oh my!
Through laughter and chatter, we plot and we weave,
The funniest tales from this nest we believe.

Riddles in the Rustling Foliage

What's round and green and swings high with glee?
The answer, my friends, is a bee in a tree!
With jests all around us, we laugh and we shout,
As nature provides us with riddles throughout.

The leaves whisper secrets, both funny and silly,
An owl's got a joke that'll make you feel frilly.
We share our best punchlines, a root-tapping cheer,
In our leafy domain, who needs a career?

Secrets of the Old Oak

In the trunk of the grand old oak,
Squirrels plot with a nutty joke.
They giggle and munch, eyes full of cheer,
While young friends laugh, with nothing to fear.

A raccoon wearing a small, silly hat,
Claims he's the king, and oh, how they chat!
The branches sway with the wind's gentle tease,
And laughter rings out, dancing with ease.

Sunlight Through the Timber

Sunlight flickers through leaves so green,
Creating shadows that dance, like a scene.
A butterfly flits; it trips and it slips,
While munching on crumbs from their snack-time quips.

The light plays tricks on unsuspecting eyes,
As giggles erupt from wearied goodbyes.
A shadowy figure known as Mister Boast,
Turns out to be just a friendly old ghost.

Dreams in the Lofted Boughs

Up in the boughs, where dreams take flight,
Imaginations soar deep into the night.
The whispers of characters, brave and bold,
Create wacky tales that never grow old.

A dragon with hiccups, a pirate with style,
They battle with laughter and grin all the while.
As moonlight tickles the heroes so bright,
They plot new escapades in the soft twilight.

Adventures Above the Ground

Adventures await in a canopy high,
Where pirates and ninjas play under the sky.
With sticks as swords and leaves for shields,
They chase the day, where laughter yields.

The knight in pajamas, riding a broom,
Finds dragons and jesters in friend's bedroom.
Through giggly tussles and bold leaps, they sweep,
Building dreams in the air; excitement runs deep.

The Fellowship of Feathered Friends

A parrot's joke, a crow's sly scheme,
In the branches, they plot and dream.
Squirrels giggle, tails in a twirl,
Nature's jesters, giving life a whirl.

With acorns flying, a comedy show,
Raccoons dance, putting on a glow.
Amidst the leaves, laughter ignites,
In this world of mischief and flights.

Feathered fables, stories unfold,
Every chirp has a tale to be told.
Mockingbirds mimic, they sing with glee,
In this treetop realm, wild and free.

Chasing shadows, they race in the breeze,
They tumble and tumble, oh what a tease!
Under the sun, a jovial parade,
In the arms of the trees, friendships made.

Fruitful Discussions and Daring Dreams

In a circle of branches, fruits gather round,
Talking of dreams, where hopes can be found.
An apple debates with a cheeky pear,
While a banana claims it's beyond compare.

Grapes chime in, all squished with fun,
Saying, "We've got juice if you need to run!"
Together they swirl in a fruity fanfare,
Plotting adventures far beyond where.

Mango brings bold ideas from afar,
While berries boast of being a star.
Coconuts nod with their husky accord,
In this orchard, wisdom is adored.

With each fruity chat, new visions ignite,
Dreams cascade like stars in the night.
From branch to branch, what a delightful team,
In the jolly chaos of nature's dream.

Ladders to the Stars

A ladder of branches, reaching so high,
As raccoons wonder, trying to fly.
Chipmunks declare, "We'll climb to the moon!"
With giggles and squeaks, they start very soon.

Up they go, in quite the fuss,
Squeezing through leaves, what a rush!
But owls chuckle from their wise old perch,
"You'll need a map for this skyward search!"

A squirrel slips, and everyone screams,
"Hold on tight to your wildest dreams!"
Swept by the wind, they're winging all around,
With laughter and cheers, they never back down.

Branch by branch, they plot the ascent,
In this wacky quest, their time is well spent.
Finding treasures in clouds, tales to share,
In the laughter of friends, there's magic in the air.

Forever Young in the Treetop Saga

In the treetops, youth is a treasure,
Where silliness reigns beyond all measure.
Old owls play games, pretending to snooze,
While young ones dart, with nothing to lose.

Every branch hides laughter and cheer,
As tune-loving bats serenade near.
A woodpecker's joke, a delightful hit,
Echoes through leaves, where wonders sit.

"Hide and seek!" calls the cheeky little chaffinch,
As squirrels scamper, and giggles clinch.
Jumping from heights with a daring glide,
In these vibrant trees, they all take pride.

Years may pass, but here time stands still,
In a world of whimsy, all hearts can thrill.
Forever young, embracing delight,
In the branches above, everything feels right.

Sanctuary Among the Stars

Up high in the branches, we play,
Building dreams in a clumsy way.
A fortress of giggles and cheer,
Where no grown-ups dare to come near.

Silly whispers of secrets we share,
With squirrels and birds, we've no care.
Nestled close in our leafy retreat,
Countless adventures await our feet.

From bickering over the last cookie,
To dodging the rain, feeling quite spooky.
With our imaginations set to soar,
Every trip up just opens more doors.

And if the winds sway us a bit,
We cling on tight, refusing to quit.
Up here, life's troubles just fade,
In our hideaway, memories are made.

Tales from the Raised Nest

Gather 'round, it's storytime,
With extra cheese and silly rhyme.
There's a dragon who dreams of cheese,
And a mouse who strums a guitar with ease.

In our nest we spin wild lore,
The cat's a pirate, and we're the crew on the shore.
Flying high on branches of fun,
With a treasure map drawn by the sun.

Epic battles with spaghetti swords,
And cookies that rain down like hordes.
Laughter echoes into the sky,
As we dodge a flying pie, oh my!

When evening falls and stars take flight,
We close our eyes, feeling just right.
Tomorrow's tales will gleam and shine,
In our raised nest, it's all divine!

Roots and Branches: A Journey

Roots grip the earth, a solid plan,
While branches sway like a crazy fan.
We built our dreams on a twisty vine,
With laughter and chaos making it fine.

A jump from the ledge, oh what a sight!
Who knew that clumsy can feel so light?
Each tumble a giggle, each scrape a tale,
As we say goodbye to slipping mail.

Birds cheer us on from above,
While we plot mischievous acts we love.
Nature our stage, it's all just right,
In our wild world, there's no end in sight.

With sticky hands, we capture the day,
Magic and mischief lead the way.
In tangled roots and a canopy grand,
We find our joy and make our stand.

Heartbeats in the Heights

High above, our hearts take flight,
Building dreams 'til the fall of night.
With leaps and bounds, we mimic the swings,
Silly dance moves, and other wild things.

A raccoon joins our late-night crew,
Cheerful chaos in every hue.
We crown him king of our leafy throne,
As laughter rumbles like a cheerful drone.

Tickling the clouds with our loudest cheer,
The moon winks at us, it's all so clear.
In our hideaway, worries just drift,
In these tree-high moments, we find our gift.

So here we hang, carefree and free,
Just a bunch of kids, nature's jubilee.
With heartbeats echoing in the heights,
We dance with stars on magical nights.

The Sanctuary of Swaying Limbs

Up in the branches, we laugh and play,
Swaying like leaves on a breezy day.
A squirrel drops acorns, a comical sight,
Dodging their bombs feels like a fight!

With snacks in our pockets, we've got a feast,
Sharing our goodies, we're all quite pleased.
The birds chirp tunes, a wild serenade,
In our leafy kingdom, we've got it made!

Swinging from ropes, our giggles take flight,
The tree's our playground from morning to night.
Below, the world's worries drift far away,
In our haven of limbs, we've come out to play!

As shadows grow long, we craft silly plans,
To scare off the raccoons with our best dance hands!
High in the treetops, we'll always conspire,
While the sunset paints gold our leafy empire.

Guardians of the Green Retreat

On our lookout post, we're kings of the trees,
Guarding the branches with the greatest of ease.
With binoculars made of a cardboard tube,
We spot all the critters, each nutty little rube!

A band of mischief, we form our brigade,
Playing pranks on the squirrels, such a jolly charade.
Each rescued chipmunk deserves a medal,
For bravery shown in our leafy-level meddle!

Alert to all dangers, we sharpen our skills,
With wild imaginations and laughter that thrills.
The trees our dominion, we stand proud and tall,
In the green retreat, we're having a ball!

When night starts to fall, we gather our crew,
Underneath stars twinkling, in shades of deep blue.
With stories and giggles, we watch fireflies zoom,
In our realm of joy, there's always more room!

Echoes of Friendship Above

In the branches we gossip, secrets to share,
With sounds of our laughter drifting through air.
The laughter ricochets from trunk to the sky,
In our treetop kingdom, we laugh till we cry!

Swinging like monkeys, we tumble and shout,
Inventing new games that we can't live without.
A leap from the swing leads to giggles galore,
Even the squirrels join the fun and want more!

With leaves as our ceiling and bark as our floor,
We spin wild tales when boredom's a bore.
The echoes of friendship, a radiant sound,
In our lofty abode, happiness is found!

As stars start to sprinkle the sky, we unite,
With dreams and our wishes taking genuine flight.
In the echoes of laughter, our world feels so bright,
Together, we conquer the cheerful twilight.

Nestled Between the Twigs

In a snug little nook, we've built our retreat,
Nestled between twigs, it feels warm and sweet.
A cozy fort made of this and of that,
With pillows and laughter, we set down our mat!

Outside, the wind whispers and rustles the leaves,
While we craft our plans for delightful mischief thieves.
An impromptu dance party, just us and the sky,
With moves so ridiculous, we can't help but cry!

Cookies all crumbled, crumbs scatter the ground,
Yet in this small space, pure joy can be found.
The sun peeks through branches, tickling our skin,
In our twig-lined haven, the fun can begin!

With shadows embracing our tiny delight,
We sing songs of silliness, hearts feeling light.
For nestled between twigs, it's more than a spot,
It's friendship and laughter, a treasure forgot!

Branching Stories Underneath

In the tree where the squirrels play,
They tell tales of a wild day.
A raccoon dressed as a queen,
Claims the acorns for her scene.

Laughter echoes from twig to limb,
As friends gather for a whim.
A parrot joins the festive round,
With jokes that astound the ground.

The wise owl hoots a funny riddle,
While the young ones laugh in the middle.
From every branch, a tale is spun,
In a world where all is fun.

So come, my friend, have a seat,
In the shade where the stories meet.
Under the leaves, so bright and bold,
This tree gives laughter, never old.

When Rain Meets the Rooftop of Leaves

Pitter patter on leaves so green,
Makes a rhythm, like a machine.
The birdies dance in drops of dew,
Wearing tiny raincoats, too.

A lightning bug flashes, takes a spin,
While frogs start a band, let's begin!
The raindrops play a silly tune,
As puddles fill up, oh what a boon!

The branch bends low with playful weight,
As the rain welcomes each small fate.
With splashes added to the song,
The world brightens, you can't go wrong.

A squirrel yells, "Look out below!"
As he jumps with a mighty throw.
Splash! A giggle, oh what a scene,
In a storm, it's all laughter and green.

Tales of the Gathering Gales

When the wind starts to roll and sway,
The tree whispers secrets at play.
A cat in a hat makes his stand,
As leaves fly like confetti, so grand.

The branches giggle, bend and sway,
When a crow thinks he leads the ballet.
With wings flapping and much delight,
They turn his performance to flight!

The gusts bring stories from afar,
Of wild ventures, near and far.
The wind takes the tales on its roam,
Whispering back to the tree their home.

So gather, my friends, 'neath the leafy dome,
Here in this space, we're never alone.
With laughter and tales the winds do bring,
We'll create a symphony as we sing.

A Nest of Wild Imagination

In a cozy nook where dreams ignite,
A nest of stories takes its flight.
With giggling critters all around,
Ideas burst forth, wildly unbound.

An ant in a cape leads the way,
As a rabbit claims it's actually May.
They throw a party, cupcakes in hand,
While a hedgehog plays in a rock band.

The clouds transform in silly shapes,
As creatures create wild escape tapes.
A floating snail with a rainbow sail,
Trading tales on an epic trail.

So climb up high, take a peek,
In this nest, imagination's unique.
With laughter that twirls like a kite,
Join us here, where dreams take flight.

Time Suspended in Timber

In a house made of wood high above the ground,
We play hide and seek and laugh all around.
The squirrels join in, they think it's a game,
As we bounce on the floor, who's winning? No shame!

A rope swing that swings with a laugh and a squeak,
We'll soar through the air; it's adventure we seek.
Time seems to pause, like a fly on the wall,
In this tree-built kingdom, we'll never grow small!

With branches as couches, we lounge and we cheer,
Each knock on the wood brings the forest's warm cheer.
There's magic in every knot, twist, and bend,
Our secret hideout, where time has no end!

So let's leap and let's tumble, let joy take its flight,
In our wooden abode, all the world feels so right.
With giggles and wiggles, the day shall not fade,
In the treehouse we crafted, our memories are laid.

Laughter in the Lofty Boughs

High in the branches, our laughter takes flight,
With each silly joke, everything feels light.
The leaves are our confetti, the sky is our stage,
As we tumble and roll, we forget any age!

With a breeze giving hugs and the sun's golden glow,
Our clubhouse of dreams is where giggles will grow.
We wear crowns of acorns and capes made of leaves,
In our lofty kingdom, we're kings and we're thieves!

The birdies applaud with their cheerful little tweets,
As we swing past the clouds, are we funny or neat?
The branches all sway with our bursts of delight,
In the high-up haven, we dance through the night!

Oh, let's tell tall tales from dawn until dusk,
Full of pirates and dragons, we'll fill them with trust.
With laughter as fuel, we'll paint the sky wild,
In the boughs so lofty, forever a child!

Stories Carved in Bark

On the trunk we carve stories with silly old names,
Of space-faring frogs and their intergalactic games.
With a knife and some giggles, we etch out our dreams,
Each twist of the bark holds our wonderful schemes.

The knots are our castles, the curls are our roads,
With every old mark, our imagination explodes.
We tell of mischief and misadventures grand,
As the wood bears our secrets with a gentle hand.

With tree sap for ink, we scribble our fate,
Each laugh a reminder that fun won't be late.
So gather 'round closely, let the tales commence,
With stories so wild, they just don't make sense!

We'll spin yarns of giants who trip over their feet,
Of ticklish old bears who find counting a feat.
The bark holds our laughter, it smiles as we write,
In the forest of stories, everything feels right!

Climbing to Imagination

Up the wooden ladder, we reach for the sky,
Every step filled with dreams, oh my, oh my!
With a hop and a skip, we're lost in delight,
As we climb to the branches, our futures look bright.

Through the leaves, we whisper our wildest ideas,
Of racing with rabbits and flying with bees.
Each twist of the trunk is a new avenue,
In this world made of laughter, anything's true!

With a treasure map drawn in chocolate and jam,
We'll seek for the gold in this treehouse we cram.
The breeze carries secrets that flutter and tease,
While we create magic with the greatest of ease.

So join us in climbing, let's reach for the stars,
As we dance through the branches, discover Mars.
In the twisty old timber, our dreams come alive,
With laughter as our guide, forever we thrive.

A Haven Among the Hues

In a tree so stout and grand,
A squirrel forms a marching band.
With acorns flying through the air,
We duck and dodge without a care.

The branches shake, the laughter swells,
As birds invade our leafy shells.
We play tag with the buzzing bees,
While ants hold court on wooden knees.

Below, the world seems far away,
With snacks and jokes to brighten our day.
Our fortress stands, so wild and free,
With every knot a memory.

The sky paints colors all around,
While we are lost in joyful sound.
A haven where our hearts can roam,
This leafy loft, forever home.

Dreams Draped in Leaves

When dreams are spun from trees so tall,
We dance like leaves in gusts that call.
A swing makes us soar, oh what a flight,
We laugh and shout from morn till night.

The sun does peek through tangled boughs,
To witness our silly, secret vows.
We'll tell the clouds our deepest fears,
With giggles masking all the tears.

A slide of bark becomes our ride,
Where laughter does not choose to hide.
With every hoot from owls above,
We scribble notes of childish love.

From tree to tree, our thoughts take wing,
In this leafy world, we rule as kings.
Our dreams are wrapped in nature's charms,
With no worry of falling into arms.

Footprints on the Rungs of Time

We climb the ladder, oh what a sight,
With socks mismatched and moods so bright.
High up we giggle, floating on air,
As clouds check in for a playful dare.

Each rung we conquer, a tale to tell,
Of secret codes and a magic spell.
We trace the years in wooden grain,
With each splinter, a laugh, a gain.

Up here, the world seems to spin so slow,
We build our dreams where wild winds blow.
Like castles made of wishes and whims,
We dance with shadows as daylight dims.

In our treebound realm, time is a friend,
Followers of fun where giggles blend.
With every step, a new adventure starts,
And footprints mark the map of our hearts.

Messages Carried by the Wind

With whispers soft and tales to share,
We write our notes and toss in the air.
Each paper plane a story spun,
As breezes laugh and start to run.

The wind becomes our faithful post,
Delivering dreams we cherish most.
With giggles trailing like fairy dust,
In friendship's bond, we all entrust.

From twig to twig, our secrets fly,
As birds above exchange a sigh.
The trees, our friends, keep watch and wait,
While the wind helps us navigate fate.

We shout our joys, we confess our fears,
As messages dance through leafy gears.
In this delightful game we play,
The wind carries dreams, come what may.

Flickers of Light Among the Leaves

In a crooked tree where kids gather,
Laughter hangs, it gets even madder.
Swinging high, we touch the sky,
The squirrels debate our daring spy.

Sunlight dances, plays hide-and-seek,
While branches sway, they start to creak.
We tell tall tales of brave old knights,
And pranks that leave us giggling nights.

Cookies crumble, crumbs take flight,
As birds swoop in for a tasty bite.
Our secret club is all aglow,
With dreams and games that only we know.

So come and join our leafy quest,
We'll build a world that feels the best.
Underneath the sky so wide,
We'll let our imaginations glide.

The Realm Above the Roofs.

Up we climb to our high domain,
Where even rain can't cause us pain.
We wave to neighbors, tease the cat,
And shout, 'Look out! We're not coming back!'

With a rope swing tied to a sturdy limb,
We swoosh through air, almost on a whim.
A perfect spot to hide our loot,
A stash of candy, oh what a hoot!

In our fortress made of twigs and beams,
We brew up mischief and wild dreams.
Our laughter echoes, a joyful song,
In our tree-top kingdom where we belong.

So take a peek above the trees,
And join us in this world that's free.
With pillows stacked and snacks galore,
Adventure waits behind the door!

Nestled Among the Leaves

A cozy nook where all can fit,
We laugh and play, and never quit.
Leaves are our ceiling, the sky our roof,
Each time we meet, we raise the goof!

Beneath a blanket of embrace,
We share our secrets, our funny face.
The wind, it tickles, it loves to tease,
While ants parade, doing as they please.

Sipping juice from little cups,
We plan our schemes, we put them up.
A treasure hunt, a daring crawl,
With giggles echoing through it all.

Nestled high, we feel so bright,
As fireflies twinkle, ending the night.
So come and join, the fun's a blast,
In our leafy haven, friendships cast!

Whispers in the Canopy

In the secret shade, whispers swirl,
As branches sway, our dreams unfurl.
Giggling softly, we trade wild tales,
Of pirates, dragons, and epic gales.

A trampoline made from woven vines,
We bounce and flip like circus signs.
The neighborhood's noise fades away,
In our leafy world, we're here to stay.

Crickets serenade as dusk descends,
With snacks and jokes, our laughter blends.
No adults allowed, it's our decree,
With freedom's spirit, we dance with glee.

So come abide in the whispering trees,
Where every moment is meant to please.
In this secret land, we reign supreme,
Among the leaves, we live our dream!

Tales from the Treetop Realm

In the treetops high, we build our dreams,
Swinging on branches, or so it seems.
Squirrels as sidekicks, they laugh and play,
Join in our mischief, hip-hip-hooray!

Snacks spill like leaves, crumbs everywhere,
Sticky fingers mess up the air.
A ladder to nowhere, a portal to fun,
Where time disappears, oh, what we've done!

A meeting of pals, conspiracies brew,
Plots of adventure, oh, how we flew!
With giggles and secrets, the daylight fades,
We scribble our stories on leafy blades.

And when we come down, we're muddy and spry,
Chasing each other, we dash and fly.
Our kingdom of joy in a treetop space,
Adventures await, come join us, embrace!

The Nest of Childhood Echoes

In our cozy nest, echoes go round,
Laughter like music, a sweet, merry sound.
With acorns for treasure, we reign supreme,
Imagining futures, bright as a dream.

A bear made of pillows, a dragon of bark,
We bravely defend 'gainst the world and the dark.
With sticks for our swords, we battle with flair,
Who knew being silly could take us so far?

When shadows grow long, we whisper and scheme,
But mom's voice calls us, shattering the dream.
We tumble and stumble, back to the ground,
With hearts full of giggles, our joy knows no bound.

Though time will march on, and branches will sway,
The nest holds our secrets, forever to stay.
In memories' arms, we'll always remain,
Two kids on a journey, forever insane!

Adventures in the Emerald Hideout

In the emerald realm where the laughter flows,
We share silly secrets where the wild wind blows.
A fort made of branches, a sanctuary sweet,
With whimsy our banner and giggles our beat.

A pet crabapple named Sir Squishy McMuff,
Declares that our lives will never be tough.
He crowns us the rulers of this leafy space,
With crowns made of daisies, we wear them with grace.

We've built a catapult for snacks on the fly,
Launching our goodies up into the sky.
And though they don't land as we planned in a rush,
We're too busy laughing; it's no time to hush!

Each day's a new tale in our hideout alive,
Where imagination blooms, and we all thrive.
In our emerald universe, we forever roam,
These silly adventures, our hearts will call home.

Shadows and Sunbeams in the Loft

In the quietest loft, with shadows that dance,
We prance like the squirrels, all caught in a trance.
Each beam of sunlight, a wizard's warm spell,
Transforming our fort into stories to tell.

We craft little worlds with the dust in the air,
Adventurers bold, in our kingdom we share.
With blankets and pillows, we travel afar,
To lands full of giggles and glittering stars.

A wicked old witch (who's really our cat),
Lurks in the corner, please watch out for that!
But we've got a plan, with a pie as our bait,
Silly little heroes against her strange fate.

As stars peek through branches, our tales intertwine,
With laughter and mischief, we toast with our twine.
In the soft, gentle glow of the night's tender grace,
We cuddle our dreams in this magical place.

Whittled Whispers Among the Pines

In a world of wood and bark,
Secrets shared with each tree's lark.
A squirrel debates with a wise old owl,
As shadows dance and the night does howl.

Pinecone parties, squirrels in hats,
Acorns rolling like playful cats.
Branches giggle, leaves all cheer,
Who knew trees could laugh so clear?

With rope swings squeaking in the breeze,
The knots complain—"Oh, pretty please!"
Branches drooping with joy all around,
Nature's comedy, truly profound.

So let's raise a toast with acorn cups,
To all the creatures and their silly ups!
At twilight's hint, the tales grow long,
In this funny forest we all belong.

The Retreat of Thunderous Trees

In the thunder's roar, the trees just shake,
Leaves quiver, and branches break.
A woodpecker plays a frantic game,
While a raccoon rolls his eyes in shame.

Underneath those mighty boughs,
A squirrel feasts, while the world's in joust.
"Who knew?"

The trees complain, "We're swaying fast!"
As the wind whirls past, our laughter lasts.

Raindrops tap dance, creating a show,
Pinecones pirouette in a dizzy flow.
Such a spectacle, no time for frowns,
As clouds mimic hats on nature's crowns.

When the storm departs, the silence is sweet,
With puddle reflections beneath our feet.
In the calm, we snicker, still filled with glee,
For these thunderous trees hold laughs, you see!

Above the World, Below the Clouds

High in the branches, we swing and sway,
With birds in suits to brighten the day.
A raccoon tries to put on a tie,
While the cheeky crow just sneezes and flies.

This lofty retreat up in the green,
Is where all the wise guys come to convene.
"Where's the snacks?" yells the hungry deer,
As whispers of munchies swirl in the air!

Below, the world seems far and small,
With ants marching like they own it all.
A butterfly winks, landing with style,
While the tree shakes laughter with every smile.

Up we go, above the ground,
To share in giggles, a joy profound.
No clouds too heavy, nor skies too blue,
In this wooden kingdom, whimsy shines through.

Chasing Fireflies in the Night

As dusk falls down, we're on the run,
Chasing glowworms just for fun!
"Did you catch one?" whispers a friend,
"Or did it fly away around the bend?"

Laughter echoes beneath the trees,
While crickets join in with joyful ease.
A raccoon's wiggle, a joyful jig,
Each firefly caught like an evening gig.

All around, the stars blink and tease,
With a moonlit glow that makes hearts pleased.
Squeaks and laughs, who knew they'd shine?
In this wild chase, everything's fine!

Fingers flicker in the golden light,
As we dance and spin through the night's delight.
"Catch me if you can!" the fireflies say,
In this enchanted game we always play!

A Haven in the Woodlands

In the branches high we play,
Building dreams by light of day.
With squirrels chuckling all around,
In our fortress, laughter's found.

We craft our forts with sticks and rocks,
Dress them up in clever socks.
While bees mock us with buzzing tunes,
We dance like silly little loons.

Our friends below all share a grin,
As we tumble, flip, and spin.
With acorn hats and pinecone crowns,
We rule the world without the frowns.

So here we shall remain for years,
With giggles chasing all our fears.
In our haven, wild and free,
Life's just one big comedy.

Fading Footprints on the Plank

Upon the rickety, creaky wood,
We dance like no one really should.
With every leap, a funny slip,
And laughter echoes as we trip.

Socks and shoes left far behind,
Footprints fading, oh so blind.
Marking trails of muddy fun,
As we race beneath the sun.

With grape juice stains and sticky hands,
We conquer all our silly plans.
Whispers float like goofy ghosts,
As we relish in our boasts.

So come along, let's sway and spin,
And let the laughter surely win.
For footprints fade but joy remains,
In our wooden paradise gains.

The Song of the Swaying Boughs

The swaying boughs hum silly songs,
A melody where laughter belongs.
We sing along with our rough tune,
As leaves dance under the smiling moon.

Chirping birds join in the fun,
As we twirl around, hearts are spun.
With each note, the branches sway,
Promising mischief every day.

In this concert of giggles and cheer,
The world feels light, nothing to fear.
Our voices rise, a joyful blast,
Making memories meant to last.

So grab a friend and sing out loud,
In our boughs, we're ever proud.
For in this song of nature's play,
We find our dreams in a silly way.

A Lullaby of Leaves

The leaves whisper tales of night,
Wrapped in dreams, oh what a sight.
Bouncing critters weave and roam,
In a lullaby, we feel at home.

Crickets chirp their sleepy tune,
Under the watch of the silver moon.
With giggles soft as feathered beds,
We'd tell stories, cheering heads.

In our cozy nest up high,
With dreams that touch the starry sky.
Grins spread wide as we drift away,
In a leaf-studded ballet.

So lay your head and close your eyes,
While the woodland sings lullabies.
For in this cradle beneath the trees,
We dance on the cusp of gentle dreams.

Sunbeams and Shadows

Up in the branches, we giggle and play,
Ignoring the chores, we dream the day away.
Swaying like leaves in a breezy dance,
Who knew that mischief could be our best chance?

Sunbeams flicker, creating a show,
While shadows tell secrets that only we know.
A squirrel peeks in, he's judging our fun,
But he can't resist, he joins in the run.

Lemonade spills, what a sticky mistake,
We laugh until we just start to shake.
Crafting our world from found bits of string,
Wishing forever, we never grow old, king!

When twilight falls, our laughter creeps out,
The trees hold our secrets, without any doubt.
Tomorrow we'll climb, for more wild play,
In a world where the sunbeams chase shadows away.

The Fluttering Pages of Memory

In our little spot where the wild things roam,
We've written our stories, the branches our home.
With paper and crayons, we doodle our days,
The fluttering pages, in sunlight, they blaze.

A dragon made of twigs, a castle of leaves,
We conquer our fears, while the tree gently heaves.
A wizard with socks, that can't stay on right,
We invent all the riddles to laugh through the night.

The breeze carries whispers of wild to the sky,
A world full of wonders where time simply flies.
Jokes about gnomes and their silly little hats,
As we roll on the floor like a couple of cats.

Memories flutter, like butterflies free,
Each one a giggle, a moment of glee.
We'll savor the chaos, the laughter, the dream,
In our tree of sweet memories, forever we gleam.

Wood and Wonder: A Retreat

High up above where the wild winds blow,
Our wooden retreat is the star of the show.
The floor creaks with stories from years gone by,
While the walls hold our laughter as time scampers by.

Two chairs and a table, a wizard's old lair,
Crafting strange potions—don't breathe if you dare!
With leaves for our cups and acorns for snacks,
We're royalty here, with no need for backpacks.

Sneaking and peeking through holes in the wood,
Imagining worlds just as we know they should.
Giggling at shadows that dance on the floor,
Why do treehouses always bring out our roar?

With forts made of pillows and dreams made of cheer,
We'll stay in this haven, no worries or fear.
In wood and in wonder, where silly does thrive,
It's a place full of magic, where we feel alive.

The Unwritten Adventures Underneath

A secret club hides beneath the old tree,
With whispers and riddles, just wait and see!
We plot out our journeys in shadows and shade,
Where the tiniest monsters are cleverly made.

Candy wrappers double as maps on the floor,
While guards made of squirrels keep watch at the door.
We're pirates of laughter, we sail through the air,
With treasure maps drawn, we'll go anywhere!

When rain starts to dance on our rooftop so sweet,
We'll gather our treasures, then make a quick retreat.
A thunderstorm party, all snacks in a pile,
We'll conquer the sky with a silly, good style!

Adventures unwritten but captured in glee,
With every wild thought, we're as happy as can be.
Beneath the old branches, our stories run free,
In the world of the hidden, it's just you and me.

Whispers Among the Branches

In a tree so tall and wide,
Squirrels chat, no need to hide.
They plot their acorn heist at dawn,
While birds sing sweet, just carry on.

A raccoon wears a pirate hat,
Says, "Join my crew!" and off we chat.
With laughter echoing in the air,
Our secret tales float everywhere.

The branches sway with every tale,
As laughter dances with the gale.
A breeze so light, tickles our toes,
And every secret freely flows.

From high above, the world seems small,
In our tree, we have it all.
With whispers soft and giggles bright,
We rule the day, a pure delight.

Secrets in the Canopy

Among the leaves where shadows play,
A secret world, we spend the day.
The owls wink with wisdom rare,
While ants march on without a care.

A bear once tumbled with a crash,
We laughed so hard, it made a splash.
He shook his head, all fur and pride,
While squirrels scampered, "Don't go wide!"

A hedgehog brought his tiny snack,
He said, "Don't touch! It's all I've got!"
With giggles shared in our hideout,
Who knew a meal could spark a rout?

Together in our leafy fort,
We gather tales of strange sort.
With secrets held and laughter loud,
In our canopy, we stand so proud.

Hideaway in the Leaves

In a leafy nook we craft our dreams,
With giggles and whispers, we plot our schemes.
The sun peeks in, a curious friend,
As we mix stories, the fun won't end.

A frog joins in, with a ribbit cheer,
He claims he's king, we laugh, "Oh dear!"
While butterflies dance, we sing our song,
In this hideaway, we all belong.

A raccoon rolls in, quite the mess,
With sticky paws, he can't confess.
His treasure trove spills on the ground,
With every shiny, new friend found.

In between the branches, joy resides,
It waves hello when we confide.
With every secret that we share,
Our hideaway breathes magic in the air.

Wooden Dreams Above Ground

Up in the branches, we stake our claim,
In a world of wood, we play our game.
With stilts and planks, our kingdom grows,
As laughter erupts like blooming prose.

A parrot squawks, "You'll never guess,"
As we hide our snacks, oh what a mess!
His feathers flash in vibrant hue,
While we navigate this world brand new.

We built a teacup ride from twine,
And claim it's better than fine dining wine.
As friends, we challenge gravity's reign,
In wooden dreams, there's no room for pain.

With every giggle, we claim our fame,
In this leafy haven, it's never the same.
So cheers to laughter that knows no end,
In our treehouse realm, where dreams descend!

The Echo of Ancient Whispers

In a nook where echoes play,
I found a chair made of hay.
It whispered tales of days gone by,
And asked me if I could then fly.

The shadows danced in silly ways,
Like two old friends in a daze.
The branches chuckled, trees did sway,
As I joined in their leafy ballet.

A squirrel perched up high to tease,
Daring me to climb with ease.
I slipped, I slid, I landed near
A mushroom that giggled with cheer.

The echoes sang, or so it seemed,
Each sound a riddle, laughing and dreamed.
In this place where giggles bloom,
I might just build a cupcake room.

Friends in the Undiscovered Heights

Up in the branches where laughter spills,
The air is ripe with silly thrills.
A parrot chats in vibrant hues,
He's got opinions on my shoes!

With every bounce and every cheer,
We're mixing snacks with fizzy beer.
A raccoon joins, declares he's king,
His crown made out of shiny bling!

The sunbeams flash, the shadows play,
As friends unite in a fun ballet.
We dance like noodles, twist and twirl,
In this high place, life's a whirl.

Together we laugh at our silly plight,
Inventing stories through day and night.
In heights unknown, we find our place,
With every giggle, we embrace.

The Elevated Diary of Dreams

In a tree where dreams take flight,
I scribble thoughts by starlit night.
Each page is full of jumbled glee,
With doodles of squirrels drinking tea.

A raccoon reads my goofy rhymes,
He laughs at my made-up times.
The owls hoot with midnight flair,
As I write tales of billy-goat hair.

The pages flutter, a soft breeze flows,
Whispers of mischief that nobody knows.
In my diary, magic spills,
With giggles and dreams, the heart just thrills.

These lofty thoughts and flying schemes,
Create a world from silly dreams.
In blinks of time, I find my grace,
In this tree, I've found my space.

Abode of Enchanted Tales

In a nook up high, with views so grand,
An abode stands, crafted by hand.
With stories stitched in every wall,
And a ceiling made of a feathered brawl.

The wind brings secrets wrapped in fun,
Of a frog who dared to outrun the sun.
Every branch grips one wacky yarn,
Tales of a cat who loved to charm.

A gnome with jokes and a laugh so loud,
He tells us tales that draw a crowd.
With each chuckle, we spin a new tale,
As squirrels practice their comedy fail.

In this abode where fancies compile,
Life is a game, and we always smile.
Each twig a chapter, each leaf a song,
Together, in laughter, we all belong.

Hues of Dawn in a Wooden Roost

Birds sing tunes that make us smile,
Coffee spills, we laugh a while.
Sunlight dances through the leaves,
As we plot mischief up our sleeves.

Branches creak beneath our glee,
Squirrels join in on our spree.
Pancakes flip, the syrup flies,
Sticky fingers, gleeful sighs.

Backyard kings upon our throne,
Pirates search for hidden bone.
The neighbor's cat gives us a glare,
While we giggle without a care.

With each shade of morning light,
We craft jokes to take to flight.
In our roost, the world's a game,
Each sunrise brings the same old fame.

Hideaway in the High Branches

Secrets whispered up so high,
A nest of laughter in the sky.
Monster sandwiches, who'll take a bite?
We giggle as the sun takes flight.

Leaping squirrels may steal our treat,
But we just laugh and find the beat.
With every leap and sticky paw,
We're plotting chaos in our law.

Trapped in our fortress, look out below,
A wild parade is set to show.
With costumes made from leaves and twine,
Actors born from nature's line.

A bubble bath with rain and joy,
A rubber duck, a ragged toy.
In our hideaway, the world feels grand,
Where laughter's born from silly plans.

Echoes of Laughter from Above

A treasure map, oh what a find!
We dig for giggles, not gold, but kind.
Old tree trunks hide our wildest tales,
Spilling secrets on the gales.

Bouncing voices, echoes cheer,
Each sound a memory we hold dear.
With echoes telling all our pranks,
We shoot the breeze, and give our thanks.

With donuts dangling from the sky,
We sip our juice and dream to fly.
A beehive buzzes our setting sound,
As we dance along the ground.

Our wooden palace sways and creaks,
Nature's whispers, laughter peaks.
In leaf-lit laughter, we forever glow,
High above, where pure joy flows.

Twilight Dreams Amongst the Twigs

The sun dips low, a perfect view,
Our wooden world now draws anew.
Fireflies join our nighttime race,
As we giggle and make silly faces.

Stars peek out with a wink so bright,
We craft our stories, full of light.
Toothpaste monsters, what a fright!
Every shadow comes alive at night.

Branching out with tales so wild,
The echoes of a playful child.
With giggles tumbling through the dark,
We write our dreams in the bark.

As twilight wraps its cloak around,
The air is filled with laughter's sound.
In our high retreat, the world sleeps tight,
While we whisper dreams until the light.

The Nest of Forgotten Moments

In a tree high above the ground,
    Where giggles and whispers abound,
A nest made of secrets and dreams,
    Teetering on life's silly beams.

A squirrel once tried to take a peek,
    But slipped and fell with a comical squeak,
While a bird sang a tune, quite absurd,
    A melody that was barely heard.

From acorns to mischief, we'd chat,
    As the wind played tricks with my favorite hat,
Moments like bubbles would rise and pop,
    In that nest where laughter won't stop.

So let's climb up this wayward tree,
    And share our tales of glee and spree,
For in this cozy and whimsical place,
    We rejoice in the joy of time's silly race.

Canopied Journeys in Timeless Tides

Beneath a canopy of emerald leaves,
    We sailed on whispers and wobbly eves,
Our ship, a plank just hanging by,
    Each journey starting with a skyward sigh.

A raccoon donned a pirate's stare,
    As if it had treasure hidden somewhere,
With snacks in hand, we danced and pranced,
    In this high up home, we laughed and chanced.

We'd chart the course through syrupy skies,
    With giggles exploding as fruit flies,
Navigating clouds like stormy seas,
    On a ship built of branches and dreams that please.

Adventure awaits with a twist and a shout,
    With funny faces that can't be knocked out,
In our treetop realm, we thrive and slide,
    On canopied journeys, it's joy we ride.

The Heart of the Hollowed Trunk

Inside a trunk, where stories unfold,
    A cozy nook, warm and bold,
Where giggles echo and echoes sing,
    A heart of laughter, always in spring.

Beetles tap danced with a playful glee,
    As I sipped my tea with a bounce in my knee,
A chorus of critters joined in delight,
    Under the stars that sprinkled the night.

Our secret spot, a magical den,
    Where dreams come to play again and again,
A raccoon chef served up snacks on a plate,
    Cooking up chaos that just couldn't wait.

With wild imaginations in full swing,
    We'd crown a king from a cardboard ring,

In the heart of the trunk, hilarity blooms,
    Creating a world where laughter resumes.

Whimsies from the Wooded Heights

From the heights of the woods, with a gleeful leap,
    We gathered tales that secrets keep,
With twigs for wands and leaves for capes,
    We fought off giants and recorded escapes.

A wobbly gnome played a fizzy flute,
    While frogs donned hats that were oh-so-cute,
With every weird twist and silly chance,
    We'd twirl and tumble in a froggy dance.

Oh, the mischief we found in each bough and bend,
    With laughter that echoed, never to end,
As squirrels recounted their grand escapades,
    In the jests of the woods, all worries cascade.

From treetop tales to the world below,
    We cast our dreams with a whimsical show,
In the heights of the woods, so wild and free,
    Where every moment creates a memory.

Adventures in the Skyward Abode

Up in the branches, we play all day,
Swinging and laughing, oh what a fray!
Squirrels throw acorns, a risky delight,
While we plot our escape, just out of sight.

Our pirate ship sails through clouds up high,
Imaginary oceans where we can fly.
With wooden swords, we duel the brave,
Chasing down shadows, the heroes we crave.

Snack time on leaves, treats we concoct,
Lemonade rivers where citrus rocks.
Our giggles echo, the wind's our fan,
While we reimagine every grown-up plan.

Jumping like frogs, we leap from our perch,
Into the grass with a playful lurch.
Gigantic adventure awaits us, no doubt,
In our skyward abode, we're never worn out!

Chronicles from the Perch

From high up above, we spy on the street,
Pretending our view is a dangerous feat.
With binoculars made from a cardboard roll,
We are the kings of our leafy console.

Whispers of gossip float up from the ground,
We snicker and nod at the antics we've found.
Mrs. Thompson dropped her umbrella again,
And Mister Smith dances like he's a hen.

We plan our escape to the candy store,
Dreaming of sweets we can never ignore.
With pockets of gumdrops and marshmallow treats,
We laugh at the thought of the sugar-packed feats.

With our trusty compass, the world is ours,
Navigating dreams beneath twinkling stars.
In the chronicles penned with giggles and cheers,
Adventures unfold through the laughter and sneers!

Harmony in the High Hideaway

In our lofty nest, we strum on some strings,
A kitty-cat band plays a tune that sings.
The tree's a grand stage, for all to behold,
With squirrels as dancers, both feisty and bold.

We harmonize loudly, but it's not always sweet,
The melody's mixed with a bark or a squeak.
But who's to complain when the moon's shining bright,
And crickets provide us the rhythm of night?

With handstands and backflips, we take the lead,
As branches sway gently, they join in our creed.
In this marvelous hideaway, all's wonderfully fine,
As laughter and music both entwine.

So here's to our shows, every giggle and cheer,
As we rock out our tunes, with no grown-ups near.
In the harmony found high up in the trees,
We're met with adventure, fun, and great ease!

Tales of the Windblown Wood

In the windblown wood, where imaginations run,
Every tree holds a tale, a riddle, a pun.
From fairies to giants, and beasts oh-so-great,
We gather them close, there's no need to wait.

A frog took a leap and got stuck in the leaves,
We chuckle and cheer as he flails and he weaves.
With stories so silly, we paint the sky bright,
Creating legends that tickle the night.

Sneaking up on a raccoon dressed like a spy,
With tacos in hand, oh how he does try!
To steal our delicious snack right from our paws,
But we'll name him our friend, and with laughter, applause.

Each moment up high fuels our tales of cheer,
In this wonderland, life's magic is clear.
So here's to the stories we share without care,
In the windblown woods, we're free as the air!

www.ingramcontent.com/pod-product-compliance
Lightning Source LLC
Chambersburg PA
CBHW072121070526
44585CB00016B/1524